The Long Haul

Books by Vern Rutsala

The Long Haul

Vern Rutsala

Carnegie Mellon University Press
Pittsburgh 2015

Acknowledgments

The American Poetry Review: "Empty Rooms," "Chickens in a Hailstorm"
The Antioch Review: "Lately"
Clackamas Literary Review: "Thieves"
The Chariton Review: "Louver"
Cloudbank: "Return to the World"
Crazyhorse: "Layers"
Free Lunch: "Summer Evenings with Dakota Slim"
Hubbub: "The Apartment Just off Burnside"
MAGGY: "Money," "How Deadshot Reed Got His Name," "The Ice Storm and After"
Michigan Quarterly Review: "Crows"
Midwestern University Quarterly: "The Sea Motel"
The Minnesota Review: "The Traveler"
Mississippi Review: "In the Columbia Gorge"
The Missouri Review: "Relatives," "Slinging Hash"
North American Review: "Junk," "An Old Street"
Northwest Review: "Hands," "Only Child," "Negotiating Curves," "Coming to the End"
The North River Press: "Body Language: The Great Blue Heron"
Oregon Literary Review: "An Old Song"
The Paris Review: "The Muses of First and Main," "Sorry Roads," "Deadpan Elegy"
Poetry: "White Water"
Prairie Schooner: "We Learned it at the Movies"
The Sewanee Review: "The History of a Grave (as Grandfather)"
Talking River Review: "At This Point"
Tar River Poetry: "Surfaces," "The History of Apples," "Her Radio," "Old Fighters at a Sports Bar," "September Arrival"
Willow Springs: "What We Owe"
ZYZZYVA: "'Finns Have Long Memories'"

"In the Columbia Gorge" was awarded the *Mississippi Review* Poetry Prize.

Library of Congress Control Number 2015932693
ISBN 978-0-88748-601-2
Printed and bound in the United States of America

10 9 8 7 6 5 4 3 2 1

Contents

to Joan

In the Columbia Gorge

I

Somehow we travel two ways at once,
going east
           while memory pages west,
uncovering the first time
we drove the old twisting two-lane
and the Gorge
             offered its dry
hills like dinosaurs, huge flanks
barnacled with boulders, looming, ready
to fall.
        Gradually, they grew trees,
then Celilo Falls roared beside us,
its platforms made of pick-up-sticks,
so precariously balanced over the torrent
while salmon seemed eager to eat
the nets.
         The road curved toward the future's
mysteries—the dream of Idaho
already fading, the old town's lights
turned off, the lake shrinking
to a puddle, even the bears in the trees
behind the little house had called in
sick.
       We never lose those first journeys—
Celilo stays locked beside us, mist rising,
water roaring.
           They unpeel from the past
like photos from the old album, glue
letting go at the corners and we meet
ourselves in the little roadster rattling
toward tomorrow
             on paper-thin retreads.
Those journeys teach us something
we can never forget. That passages

are never easy, taking time and patience
however impatient we are. There is no
true arrival without earning it with some
minimum wage of the spirit.

II

                              Dams blindsided
Celilo and now windsurfers
have taken over while others
fish from boats dotting the surface
between the whitecaps.
                              How do they
differ from the ones who used nets?
For one, the rich always take over
actions they know meant everything
to the poor—fishing, hunting—
and without imagination they call it sport.
But what about
                    the salmon—they seem
to be deserting the cause,
refusing to hold up their end
of the deal. Have they forgotten
their way? Did the old stories fade
in their guts making them forget
where they came from, the return
plucked from their genes?
                              No, mainly
they die somewhere else thanks to our
cleverness.
                    But today we return
greeting the selves we once were—
the dreams, our private histories
lost somewhere on the ancient road
like an old shoe.

III

> The first time
we came this way the siren of a war
called us and we have that again,
locals from Guard outfits in the little
towns are in the desert now.
We even see a few tattered yellow
ribbons—but no one talks of war
in the diners, mainly it's fishing
and weather, subjects safely
beyond the teeth of history.
>
> > But war
is always there—about to happen,
happening, or ending
> > > and about to start
again.
> The older the wars the more
just they seem though they've always
brought an empty whisper to our houses
and for survivors cold sweat nightmares
plowing the surface like old bits
of shrapnel.
> > We journey back
to our version of that war—for children
it was rumor and adventure ahead
on the highway. But there was grayness,
too, that seemed to settle on us
like fog as if that were the real end
of the glory the Gorge promised.
> > > The past
is always there, just over
your left shoulder
> > > > but you can never
glance back fast enough to catch it.
It has some quicksilver speed, some
corner of the eye evasion even though

those you once loved are somehow
still there in lost words ground into
the road, those questions
                              they will never
answer like phone lines
                              gone dead in a storm.
Once again the little roadster
heads toward the war that somehow
paused while we drove west.
It waited for us in Portland,
with the drab darkness in
the grim apartment.
                        Mostly
it meant my mother going

to work at four
                    and the strangeness
of eating supper with my
father, her chair vacant,
the whole apartment emptier
with her absence—was it
some omen?

IV

              Traveling through
the Blues one April we hit snow
and raced it down the mountains,
no chains in the trunk, our tires good
but ignorant of snow.
                          Then Baker
City announced itself off

to the right, huddled with its
trees and steeples.
                        We could
have stopped but felt the storm

peering over our shoulder.
In the old days the town
was just called Baker—
a solid no-nonsense name
but it must have made later
Rotarians uneasy so they added
"City" to give their egos
a boost. (Of course they said
it was the original name, implying
a kind of booster's honesty
in their affectation. It's worth
a tight smile at least.)
We waved
                as we passed—
it's where my mother was born.
There's a picture of her
in the album—a chubby
towhead of three.
After her first biopsy she
wanted to see the town
again, touching base, I guess,
bringing things full circle.
She and my father drove there
that summer.
                        It was more
than a threatening storm
that waved us by that day.

V

Traveling east as our old selves
backtrack their way behind us
like ghosts,
                we dream the Gorge
again through their eyes—
that taut memory of discovery
scrolling out like a vapor trail

of mica.
 They seem so many
miles away yet still with us
as if just outside the windows
making the air inside
the car close as the great river
sings its long arias of water
beside us and Celilo Falls returns
just as the old twisting road
repaves itself into being.
 We hold
our breath for the wrong turns
our parents took, not sure we
can avoid them now though once
we thought them foolish.
That foolishness matures in us
now as the map forgets the route
as we eke our way over all
those years between reliving
all the lost discoveries
that mint themselves new again.

Summer Evenings with Dakota Slim

After supper the nozzle of the hose
scattered rainbows in the garden,
the sun near the horizon, his rolled
cigarette wedged in the corner
of his mouth. He liked to swamp
those vegetables knowing how
thirsty summer made them feel.
His thirst was great, too.
Chores kept his mind off
the downtown taverns where
his buddies seemed to call
his name with their boozy
invitations.
              Chopping kindling
like a sculptor, he just tossed
the chunk on the block to make
it stand and hacked away
without even holding it in place.
He chopped so fast the axe
became a silver blur.
              He taught
me how to carve shavings that got
the big cookstove burning at dawn,
but made sure I put my free
hand above the spot I whittled.
Always cut away from you,
he said. I loved the curls that
appeared, the straight wood
peeling off in question
marks.
          While watering he never
said much, eyes far off—all the way
to Canada maybe or possibly
he just ground his teeth on
the gristle of one more day
of his dusty sobriety.

He always
drained and coiled the hose
with care and finished up
by pulling a few weeds
with his thick fingers before
going into the kitchen for his
tenth cup of coffee of the day.

The Muses of First and Main

Moths bat their brains to powder
against the streetlight

on the corner of First and Main
where the old men gather—

suspenders tight on their bellies,
skin pink as a baby's

where they've just shaved.
They have all the time in the world

in their big pockets
as they smoke and spit judiciously.

Silence is just fine, too,
though it makes the real card

among them nervous
so he fidgets out a joke

they've heard a thousand times before.
But they laugh their

gargling rich laughs
before settling back

into the luxury of summer twilight
on the corner they own, recklessly

drawing on their one great
source of capital, time.

Nothing intervenes. They have no
families calling them to supper

to swell or break their hearts.
They are right where they want to be,

aristocrats of their evening corner,
smack-dab lords of First and Main.

Relatives

You pull away from them, they drift
from you, becoming a chance
phone call, a Christmas card
you always meant to answer.
You hear of one, a man you never
liked, reduced to sitting
in a deck chair in California
while that crackpot uncle
keeps sending you religious tracts
and praying ominously for your
soul. His letters are always threats
but they come less often now.
Others just turn up, ancient
cousins of your dead father
suddenly enflamed with family
passion. But you have none
and want none. It is all so old,
so depleted, so restricted to the dreams
conjured by the album. You want
the past there with its fading
evocations of scattered shadows
and drift, but a card from
a nearly invisible great aunt
uncovers memories you thought
were lost of picnics and sun
and you say, yes, you will
drive to see her in the nursing home
but you never do. The past
is too far away to reach by car.

Sorry Roads

Their sorrow is something like
buyer's remorse. They chose
their paths but now regret it,
realizing—too late—they could

have gone to the seashore
or forests of sweet pines.
But there is one I like, ignored
by engineers, looking like

the sorriest of them all. It's off
the map in Idaho and rises
and falls, goes over rickety bridges,
seems almost to lose its way

completely but finally staggers
into the yard of the old farm
one sepia evening, the years
peeling back like stripping bark

from a willow. It's the time
the old man cleared the land
for the homestead and hammered
the old house together

with his bare fists.
Tonight I catch the scent
of sawdust, the new siding still
white as stripped willow.

Return to the World

Rolling back over all that old geography,
the tires of the old Chevy—
the one we kept up on blocks by the shed—
remembers potholes and gravel
and the blind curves leaping out

with their dangers. Lake Fork
was where we used to turn—that name
joining the others with strangeness:
Lardo, Sylvan Beach,
somewhere up the line: Riggins.

An aura hovered around those names
giving them the resonance of church bells.
No others have meant so much
or been so intricately strange,
still lingering at the edges of dreams.

Now I drive around the lake,
the Chevy's wooden steering wheel
thick and stiff in my hands.
We pass Little Lake
where it crawls off into the scrub pine,

Indian Village, the summer cabins of the rich,
much nicer than our shacks.
I hear their glossy boats rip paths across the water,
towing bronze skiers bouncing over the wakes,
looking carefree as cruise ship brochures.

Had they the wit those summer visitors
would have told us to eat cake,
and we in turn would have happily
stormed their Bastille if we knew where it was.
Mostly we watched them stroll along Main Street,

never looking at us, probably laughing at the yokels
behind our backs. Winters, though, we never minded
when high school kids broke into their cabins
and drank all their leftover booze.
Before Labor Day they drove their big cars south

on the roads that seemed barred to us.
I steer the Chevy along that road now
and feel the no-nonsense of winter
gathering behind Brundage Mountain,
remembering how snow

called the rich back in their fancy boots
and skis to make sure we were behaving ourselves.
Our only consolations were the plaster casts
some wore on their legs, elaborately
endorsed by all their friends.

But it is suddenly late and I can't go
any farther. The old Chevy labors back
to its place by the shed,
climbs up onto its blocks,
and sinks with our history into the weeds.

September Arrival

Summer drains from all the plastic pools
and evenings spread out ahead of us like the highways of childhood,
paved with impatience, too long. And they go nowhere.
We wait. We observe.

The old men who walk dogs go by carrying canes,
wearing spotless straw hats,
their dogs clipped and brushed with feet so delicate
they don't even touch the sidewalk,

leashes like the strings on balloons.
At precisely ten minutes after sundown lights go on,
a time designated—you might say demanded—by the Weather Bureau,
and the blue glow of the TV screens attracts eyes

the way a cold glass gathers moisture form the air.
And the stubborn weather goes on ignoring the schedules of courses
we advise it to take. Children practice war in fading light,
their feet stirring the first fallen leaves.

Long ago we strapped our hearts to our wrists
and set out on our journeys. This is the place we came to,
following twilight to see how far it goes. But it goes nowhere,
it just gives up, surrendering to some law

that demands our surrender, too, each night.

An Old Street

This dream takes us to an old street
where clothespins and tinkerers
counted. There was that way
of hanging out washing—

pins in the mouth, hiking a shirt
up on the line and making it
stick at the shoulders like a target.
Someone in the garage everyone

called Pops was elbow deep
in grease or had his vise gripping
something so hard you knew
it had to break. Everyone was

a vet, old duffel bags in closets,
and many still wore their old
black low quarters—the ones
that never seemed to wear out.

Fathers and sons knew the drill
though it was peace time
for the sons and the fathers
never talked about the war.

And there were other mysteries:
polishing the car with chamois
skins, mowing the lawn, and all
that tinkering in the garage where

tools dozed on pegboards
and there were never enough
clothespins for Monday's wash,
waving its strange helpless

signals all afternoon long.

The Cradle of Civilization

No Tigris or Euphrates flowed
anywhere near where I
grew up. I remember swampy
land and skunk cabbage

a little footbridge always
threatening to give way,
sagging like a clothesline
when you stepped on it.

Looking down you saw
water bugs balanced
on the surface like the pins
our teacher floated in

her special glass to show
us surface tension.
We gagged and nodded
our understanding.

In the swamp I remember
killdeer and tadpoles
and bent underwater grass,
the silt so smooth you

thought you might sink
forever like the quicksand
at Saturday matinees.
But always the pert swiftness

of those bugs and how right
their swiftness seemed.
If only we could move
that fast, skaters on

the world's surface!

But there was the frog's
tongue too, how fast
it peeled the bugs off

that surface tension
without a ripple, and then
how deliberately snakes
caught and gagged those

frogs so slowly down.

Hands

My father's are the first I remember—
thick fingers, knuckles bulging, calloused,
and nails like frosty bottle glass.
My fingers were so small,

the nails just pink chips.
At such times—four or five—
you think of growing up, of someday
hauling around ten beefy fingers

but can't imagine it ever happening—
that future the other side of the cosmos.
And I noticed other hands—how you seemed
to have to earn them with hard work—

uncles', family friends', my grandfather's.
But I had no work to do
and I knew I would never grow up,
time passed so slowly. How could I ever

win such blunt fingers, such nails?
How could I ever shake such hands
and join their rough brotherhood?
Their grips were sure to squeeze my fist

to putty or, worse, take it easy on me,
consigning me some lesser role
in life, some limp office worker
with hands too weak for saws and hammers,

fingertips fit only for keyboards.
Over the years though, I found a few callouses
and at fourteen could palm a basketball.
And one summer on a job I hated,

I learned to pound tenpenny nails
with a single blow. But it had all
taken so long—those hands I envied
now grown too palsied to shake.

Her Radio

Compared to hers our little Sears
portable was like a leaky skiff
next to one of those gleaming
Chris Crafts the rich people

hauled to the lake every summer.
(Remember how those motors
purred and chuckled by the dock
just before plowing deep wakes

across the water?) And hers had
that green cat's eye in the middle
of its forehead, blinking its mystical
light when she flipped it on,

leaned back in her platform rocker
and lit her Pall Mall. Even the war
news sounded better on that great
brown console, Murrow's

and Kaltenborn's voices deeper
and more elegant, making it seem
that everything would work out well.
On our little white radio the news

was often chewed by static, making
us unsure of how the war would
turn out, the voices jumpy,
the interference sounding like

gunfire not that far away.

Only Child

In your childhood you were
   too poor to have imaginary
friends—they belonged to
   rich classmates with patios
and dining rooms and family
   silver. What you had was
a kind of longing as you
   played by yourself near

the woodshed or at the spongy
   edge of the swamp among
skunk cabbage and weeds.
   Watching the water bugs dart
you saw your own sketchy
   face rippling on the murky
surface and wanted someone
   just like you, the ultimate

companion to share your
   loneliness, your longing was
for a twin. You sometimes
   dreamed of her but awake
you never talked to her,
   that was a luxury for the rich—
a kind of arrogance as they
   ordered their invisible

companions around like
   servants, a kind of lazy
indulgence. For you to talk
   to your twin would have
broken the spell. It was enough
   to know she was out there
somewhere. You knew
   you would meet some day.

Money

*. . . the art of becoming "rich" . . . is not absolutely . . . the art of
accumulating much money for ourselves, but also of contriving
that our neighbors shall have less.*

—John Ruskin

*Society is made up of two great classes: those who have more
dinners than appetite, and those who have more appetite than
dinners.*

—Chamfort

*The law, in its majestic equality, forbids the rich as well as the
poor to sleep under bridges . . .*

—Anatole France

I

In this season of foreclosures
                              I see my grandfather
riding steerage to America,
                              his wife's face already
a blur behind Finland's icy windows.
                              For seven years
he gandy danced across the plains and gouged
copper from Minnesota's dirt, digging for enough
cash to buy her a ticket.
                    And she came, the disgraced
daughter of a landowner, leaving her shame
at home for marrying a field hand.
                              Money is always
the issue in this season of bankruptcies.
The bank gobbled up their beautiful farm, a loss
so hard it planted a killer pneumonia
in his lungs and chased her wild to the asylum
in Orofino.
            Just a couple of things money can do.
For three years my father sweated off

the debt and wound up with a hundred
dollars for his trouble.
                              His brother and sister,
hissing through their bad teeth, accused
him of cheating them.
                              This is another of money's
fancy tricks.
                Turning families inside out,
turning love upside down, ratcheting hate up
notch by notch.
                              Bits of the farm rise in the dark—
the whispering floors, the attic with a few
cast iron toys, all broken, the swampy ground
beside the stream and the fading smell of livestock
in the barn after they were led away one by one,
hooves echoing on the road to town.
                                        They still
wander in my dreams—the damp rooms,
splintered boards by the porch, the flimsy
bridge across the irrigation ditch.
                                        We're all
ground under the heel of money—the heel
pressing our wallets flat as roadkill toads.
For some though dollar signs confer
the odor of grace,
                        but for the rest of us
it's just an absence like the place where
a tooth was pulled that somehow left
its ache behind.
                The lost farm hovered
over my father all his life, the Depression
waiting to jump on him
                              with all fours, sucking
his spirit dry acre by acre.

II

You have a different
feel for money if you've spent hours
walking the pavement looking for change
or collected bottles to buy a bad sandwich,
all too familiar with the "have not" side
of the equation
                    while the "haves" swam
by in their cars like yachts, sneering
through their tinted windows
amid the smell of fine leather
and cash.
          I'm sure they laughed at such
scuffling for coins, making jokes at my
expense about how old Rockefeller rubbed
it in by handing out dimes.
                              For my mother
and father the Depression—not prosperity—
always loomed just around the corner,
longing to claw every last thing from their
hands—
        even the sagging couch, the teetering
kitchen table, the paper-thin rug. It made
them gun-shy with their pennies, always
settling for factory seconds, the sad bargains,
the half-price irregulars.
                            Those cars that made
me invisible aimed toward houses of vast
ease—money allows your skin to touch
only soft surfaces, silks and sables, cashmere
and velvet.
            Such comfort an insulation
that wedges miles between the rich
and the poor,
              weather only a rumor to them,
weather that finds such easy access

into the houses of the needy, summer
or winter coming in with ease,
                                        lives always
at the wrong temperature, too hot
or too cold.
                    But weather fidgets at the back
doors of the rich, beggars waiting
for a handout, never invited in.
                                        The routine:
counting pennies, scrounging bottles and lying
awake aching for the month to end
as visions of the next paycheck—just out
of reach—dance in your head.

III

                                        For those
who have it, money goes deep and they're
sure the phrase is wrong—it's not the deserving
poor, it's the deserving rich,
                                        those born
on third base thinking
                                        they'd hit a triple
while the rest of us eke our way to first
with a scratch single and maybe get to second
but more likely we'll die on first,
third beyond our wildest dreams. A home
run? You've got to be kidding.
                                        But the rest
of us have had a few sips at the trough,
the easy breathing
                                        of money in the bank,
knowing for once your check won't
bounce.
                    But then the insulation goes
thin and you're back
                                        in the dark, staring.

And even the rich feel the flutter of absence
in their bellies, the market's catastrophic
swan dive, the absence stealing their
thick carpets and towels, the leathery
smell of their cars gone rancid.
                              Still we keep
at our stupid dreams, our impossible
lotteries, our magic windfalls hurtling
through our nights, twisting our days
paralytic or worse,
                    always looking for
the way out that never comes.
                              And the answer
is no answer, the hope is no hope
and the last disaster is mortality which
can't be bought off.
                    So the luggage we carry—
scuffed, half empty, handles biting into our
palms—our hopes inside
                        flaking to powder.

IV

Oh we pretend we know what we're doing
with money but of course we don't—
no one does. It's a game without rules.
Sometimes it flows in
                        but panic flashfloods
sweep it away to someone else—those
with all the toys who are so careful,
so judicious with their tips and so generous
with their advice for chefs
                          and dubious
about beggars, sure they'll just spend
handouts on booze as they drain another
bottle of expensive wine.
                        The big cars

keep swimming by, some with skis
on top showing that for them there's
always an elsewhere on tap—the mountain
chalet, the seaside cottage
                                while we're
squarely stuck in our round holes
looking at the same walls and waiting
for the paper to peel, the cracks to appear.
We go nowhere and even if we try
to think of travel most days
even bus fare is hard to come by
and where would we go anyway?
We would freeze in the mountains
and on most beaches they roust you
when you try to sleep in the sand.

Coda

As you drive by toward your gated
houses you see them on street corners
slouching or bowing back and forth
too fast like those bobble heads
in the back windows of old cars.
But if you think of them as "Them"
you're wrong. They are you as they
crawl into your backseat. They bang
their heads against your headrest,
they follow you into your house,
limping and nodding yes yes yes
over and over and make you count
all the empty bottles in their grocery
carts as you try to fall asleep.

Abundance

She had the first freezer
in the neighborhood and it
was always full. When young
she had gone hungry once too often

so she wanted to be ready
for the next famine
hovering just over the horizon,
whispering *Dust Bowl, Dust Bowl.* . . .

Neighbors smiled behind her back
as she struggled home with huge sacks
from the supermarket day after day,
filling every cranny of that freezer.

But she wasn't a miser—
more a Lady Bountiful really—her table
always loaded to the point
of collapse for special dinners.

And, face it, most of us know
the satisfaction of the full bottle
and the groaning board, the bursting
larder and the full gas tank,

just as we carry a Mother Hubbard
inside us, fearing the bleak sadness
of empty cupboards without
even a single bone for the poor dog.

Chickens in a Hailstorm

After such long domestication
do you suppose chickens learned
all their bad habits from us?

The whole pecking order business
for instance. Were they once
quick-witted and grew stupid

copying our ways? That time
in Idaho when the hailstorm hit,
Uncle Bob had to run out

and shoo the hens into the coop
otherwise they would have stood
around looking up foolishly

until the stones killed the whole
flock one by one. They didn't
learn that from us, did they?

Showing some wit himself Bob
put the wash basin on like
a helmet to save them. When he

came back in the basin was
so dented it looked like it had
been through a war. But the hens

were clucking on their roosts
congratulating each other
on how smart they were

to come in out of the storm.

Old Fighters at a Sports Bar

Scattered among the young with their
baseball hats on backwards, the old-

timers sit who still remember the real
Sugar Ray. A few even have faint

memories of hearing the second
Louis-Schmeling fight over speakers

at lumberyards and parking lots.
All that history coils in their bodies

as they watch tonight's fight on TV.
See how they feel their way into

the action, see their wincing gestures
as they bob and weave, flinch at jabs

and grip the chairs holding their hands
in place. It's as if they were kept

in restraints, their moves caught
short in lurching spasms in their

forearms and quick tensions in their
wrists as they work through

the bout round by round, their bodies
giving sketchy versions of the action

in the ring. A tic flares up near an eye
as one slips a hook, blinks at a one-two,

muscles remembering how it used to be.

Junk

Everyone loves the guys who bring
the heat, fast and a little wild,
glowering before the high kick
and delivering one that puts

the batter's foot in the bucket
or, worse, makes him bail out.
But the one who throws junk,
who puts nothing at all on the ball,

seems un-American with his
nibbling subtlety, bringing that
slow stuff even Little Leaguers
could smash as the ball creeps

toward the plate looking naked
as an egg. Yet the best rarely
get a clean hit off him—the ball
dipping inside or out, wherever

they least expect it, nipping
a corner or just above the letters.
If they do hit a pitch it dribbles
down the third-base line like

a bad bunt or pops up to short,
occasionally flies lazily to left.
And the pitcher doesn't look
the part—big as a football player

but a little dumpy, belly bigger
than it should be and with
a schoolmaster's face, pursed lips
and rimless glasses. Sometimes batters

try to bunt on him but he moves
off the mound cat-quick, scoops up
the ball and teases them by making
them run it out before throwing

his only fastball of the day.

We Learned it at the Movies

Walking home through the dull colors
   of our neighborhoods, picking bits
of popcorn from our teeth, we did
   what our teachers taught us—walking
and smoking and licking our lips
   with aloof disdain—like Bogart.

But coiled beneath the brilliant screen
   we felt a darkness spinning with
menace. Beautiful women like
   Carole Landis killed themselves—Gail
Russell, so pretty and misty-
   eyed we all wanted to give her

comfort, and when she died we ached
   over those dark smudges under
her eyes but caught hints from movie
   magazines—mad binges, crazy
full-bore drives, wild parties. Like trains
   rushing into tunnels, fade-outs

in bedrooms, everything seemed to
   happen offstage. We heard of how
decent-looking Tom Neal brawled with
   Franchot Tone over Barbara
Payton. Under that steel helmet
   of hair she seemed too cool to pull

out such passion. We were learning
   faster than we cared to, actors
squeezing crazily off the screen
   into real life. Someone gunned down
Our Gang's silly Alfalfa—goofs
   could die, too. But we kept going

week after week, feeling the world
    shrink and lose color as we walked
home, knowing a lot more went on
    behind those plots, some ranging and
skirling in the world's bleak alleys
    the movies only hinted at.

And we hadn't even reached James
    Dean or Sal Mineo, Judy
or Marilyn who blazed the trail
    rock stars later followed into
the tabloids. We found out that those huge
    delectables were delicate

as moths and how behind the screen
    there were torn and mangled lessons
we'd never understand
    even if we sat through every
double feature until
    the film burst into flames.

An Old Song

Tonight starts with the old song:
Most of our houses are gone,
razed to make way for malls
and freeways, just dreams now

hovering above parking lots
or buried under highway thunder.
It's the American way, destroy
and then build, build then destroy.

There are nights though like this
when you try to remember just
what those lost rooms were like,
try to inhabit them again,

to move the old furniture back in
and repopulate that arid past.
You spend whole nights combing
that dead landscape like going

through pants pockets one last
time before giving them to
Goodwill, looking for coins
or some forgotten treasure.

But tonight, pretending to walk
in the woods you come across
one house—abandoned, yard
gone wild, nearly erased by

the crazy growth around it.
On one side the roof has caved in,
the brick chimney scattered
like old dominos falling into

high weeds. Inside, the floor
is wavy as rushing water, broken

through and dangerous, walls
bloated where storms barged in,

ceilings hanging down like ancient
tents. And all this, decrepit,
nearly gone to zero, is an exact
picture of memory, no edited

version of your past, simply what
memory is, without embellishing
lies, simply this shattered
debris utterly beyond despair.

Negotiating Curves

I look for this one in daylight,
following Sunnyside Road
along its old green way
toward home, but like so
many American roads it
has lost its way. It's now
vague as the Oregon Trail
chewing grass somewhere
off to the east. Even the corner
I always turned is gone,
a severe new curb tells my
tires so with a thudding No.
And that thud's message
is clear: America has done
with nibbling, another mall
swallowed my old street
whole—every house and tree,
every little gravel memory
gulped down, those twilights
of guitar music, every sigh
and sound of love edited out
by a bulldozer's blue pencil.
I sense all those years scraped
flat and remaindered under
asphalt, everything coming
down to this country's final
either/or—Sale/No Sale.

The Apartment Just off Burnside

After all that burning light in Idaho
The apartment was dark as a cave,
Flimsy ivy struggling over windows,
The sun winking between the leaves.

The apartment was dark as a cave,
WWII lurking just beyond the ivy,
The sun winking between the leaves.
Winter taught the rooms to lose their color.

WWII lurking just beyond the ivy,
Blackout curtains made the night grow deeper.
Winter taught the rooms to lose their color.
The war seemed both far and near at once.

Blackout curtains made the night grow deeper—
Inside every looming shadow I felt fear.
The war seemed both far and near at once.
Our enemies were like mist but very close.

Inside every looming shadow I felt fear
Seeping under all the closet doors.
Our enemies were like mist but very close.
Fear was even in the food we ate.

Seeping under all the closet doors
The shadows launched their sneak attacks.
Fear was even in the food we ate.
Our companions were dread and darkness.

The shadows launched their sneak attacks
As we inched our way through the night.
Our companions were dread and darkness
After all that burning light of Idaho.

Coming to the End

By now our last best hope
is a broken muffler
scraping its brains out
along the road, giving
our anthem a new music.
We know the frontier
is out to lunch for good
and we stand in its
stale prop wash, our
streets of gold become
just buckling tar. There's
no way back—experts
at amnesia have paved
the trails with souvenirs
from Hong Kong
and rubber checks.
It's just as well.
Going back would
only stir up that old
arthritis in our souls
and rattle tin cups for
those lost cellars where
even the potatoes
have gone blind.

Sight Unseen

Though you were never born
I think it's time you shared
a little of the grief
                    life turns up
on hot summer nights like this.
My problem of course is that
you never knew
                    heat or cold
or grief or for that matter
summer—but I've got to jump
into this
              before the morning sun
makes me lose my nerve.
First, I dreamed of you,
daydreamed mostly
                    and talked
about you with our mother
before you were never born.
You were due in October
but something went wrong
and you disappeared forever.
Guilt and grief swam together
when I remembered
how I hated
              the idea of you
at first and then came to love you
sight unseen.
                    But then that
darkness erased you from
my life—
              and of course it was
all my fault somehow
for that early hate and fear
of change. Sometimes I still feel
that—right now for instance—
but that was all those years ago.

Just think of what you've missed!
You could be nearing fifty,
fat and bald,
             could have a job
you hate and the monkey
of a mortgage on your back.
You might even hate your older
brother,
        obscurely blighted
by the fact of his life.
Or it could go
             the other way—
the blight could be mine,
sibling rivalry carried into
a pouting middle age.
But to get down to cases—
what you missed.
             For starters,
our parents' deaths.
             When our
mother died you would
have been in college
or the army.
             You could have
flown home and waited
in the hospital's dim light,
could have heard her rough
breathing in your own throat,
could have cried in rage
with me.
             Cried, too, when our
father died two years later,
all light gone from his
blue eyes.
             (My problem persists.
I assume you know color
and life, assume you know

wards and dim light—I know
you know death.)
                        But maybe
your presence in the world
would have changed our story
somehow,
            postponed the grief
at least. Maybe the thing
that made them die would have
detoured for years because
of the way
            you laughed or cried
or craned your neck or lied
with charm. Maybe you would
have taught all of us some secret
way to revise the script for good
with more sunlight and lives
so brilliant
            they could never stop.
Of course everything may have
twisted even darker
                        because of some
highway curve you missed
at sixteen, but I doubt it.
Sight unseen I have faith in you.
You would have driven fast
but well.

        Questions keep churning
up but let me settle for the big one:
Is it truly better never to have been
born?
        But, sadly, this is no dialog.
It's a letter to an unknown
address inside a summer night.
Forgive the grief
                        I've tried to make
you feel tonight—for now I ask you

only to feel the trembling earth
and with it war and hunger,
the disease of being human,
but feel too
                    the seasons
and light through the leaves,
feel windy days and the sea
in winter,
                    and food and drink
and love, this particular hopeless
love with nowhere else to go.

The Sea Motel

The irritable Pacific,
                     hungry for boardwalks,
changes coastline maps
                      tonight and I feel
it wants us tallied
                  with each crusted
doubloon found in lost
                    galleons, with each
dying fish pressing
                  the fern outline
of its bones in rock.
                   Someone is singing
in another room—
                a song of ashcans
and dead children's toys.
                   Traffic goes by
bound for the ice
                  of Alaska, high beams
moving like the flashlights
                    of movie ushers.
Words are muffled under
                  rubber treads
but he goes on.
                 A shoe clerk gone mad
perhaps, singing of
                  Triple E or maybe
a sailor chanting
                  of something at home
in sea caves that
                  sings even without
listeners.
            All day I've been thinking
of flowers wilting
                  after funerals—
no brightness left
                 but foil paper

and ribbons, petals
                    turning brown
as tobacco, stalks
                    thinning in an empty
house. Of this
                    and the long afternoons
invalids spend
                    writing thank you notes
to sunshine chairmen.
                              The singer nearby
is an Irish tenor.
                    I imagine him waiting
beside the ocean
                    for his vogue to return,
sheet music quietly
                    entering the public
domain.
          Tonight my pen favors
the stunted
                    and peculiar, morning will
reveal the tree outside
                    my window—
bent back and dwarfed
                    by salt wind
from the sea—
                    and sitting in the rain
just up the highway
                    from Coos Bay,
I'll watch it bend
                    another fraction
toward the Rockies.
                    Now a warm
summer rain soothes
                    the coast's battered
skin like a hand
                    smoothing out pained
wrinkles on a sick forehead

                              or someone
trying in a lonely ward
                    to kiss away
a buried cancer.

The History of a Grave

You wait back there somewhere
in that little graveyard
under the wooden marker—
nearly all your meaning locked
in your dead children's
hearts. By now there's probably
a dam in that valley
and your grave is under water.
It seems fitting—years ago
they moved your house
to a site we never found—
and if you still think
maybe you would think
it was the Baltic surging
above you and that you never
made it to America, all that
work just a restless dream.
Mention of you always
drew pain into my father's eyes
even when he laughed
about your ways. A hard
man, he would say. Hard.
I have the old pictures—
You look a little like Gorky—
and my dwindling supply
of stories, stories about
a stranger finally, stories
no one can verify now.
Those who told them are long
dead and you died when
I was ten months old,
an Idaho winter planted
in your lungs. Images
of the farm flash by
like slides and there
are times I almost see you

standing there beside
the unfinished barn.
Where did they move
the old house? Is your
grave truly gone for good?

The Ice Storm and After

Last year began with ice,
    each twig artfully sheathed
and the cold rose like water.
    First the ankles, then the knees.
It was not a good sign.
    Nor was it delightful to hear
trees exploding like gunshots.
    Even walking was a problem.
Remember that trip to 7-Eleven?
    How many days did it take?
But when the heat came
    back on we basked in that
sudden Florida of contentment.
    Later, the chainsaws came.
We heard their whine
    for weeks. There was a dark
message in that sound,
    that hysteria, that growling
hunger for stumps.
    And where would it end?
It had the mindless tone
    of the letter of the law.
It was the music of ends
    and means. Tree after tree
became fireplace size
    because it was easier
that way. The music
    was the soundtrack
of committee meetings,
    the trumpet blare
of the big shot's memo,
    a lyric chorus of the worst
singing with passionate
    intensity of how their ends
always justified their means.

Slinging Hash

When she turned up we heard
those spike heels first,
clicking loud enough to throw
sparks and then she burst in
scattering boxes of chocolates
and perfume, looking like
a million dollars with a smile
that could melt even our town's
hard hearts. There was usually
a man along—that visit's uncle—
tall and silent, fairly free with
his quarters. She had pulled free
of town by slinging hash
at truck stops from Idaho
to California, winding up in L.A.
which seemed just far enough
for her. Far enough at least
to allow these yearly visits
that let her keep her distance.
She was a knockout and always
had matching purse and gloves
and the first real false eyelashes
we ever saw. Her luggage
matched too and those bags
were bountiful with the spoils
of her tips—shirts, ties, belts
and bottles of aftershave, model
planes. It was like Christmas
in July. She forgot no one
and those uncles spiced up
the town's dull gossip for
a month or two—just the ticket
our nosy rubbernecks needed
to get them through the summer.

Louver

Back home after weeks at the beach
you long for that sound again
and lean into the autumn air
but hear only your old familiars:
trains coupling and uncoupling in the far yards
or riding low out of town.
Even so the night seems good.
The sidewalk cracks have learned a new beauty
and the leaves leaning
toward winter now seem
thick and bright and immortal.
And the sea is still with you,
sighing and pumping its long regrets
so that far-off cars
whisper their tires like surf
and a quick breeze scents the street with brine.
Some louver in space and time
is ajar and you slip through.
You walk with one foot on wet sand—
water seeping in at each step—
the other on cement
that shifts and takes your prints.
Near home these parallels
braid and cross and veer away
then twine again.
Grass and seaweed mix
and trains set out to sea.

Body Language: The Great Blue Heron

Shoulders hunched, looking
down like someone thinking

deep or unpleasant thoughts—
bounced checks, an old grief

flickering alive again—
he gives his swampy twin

the eye, rippling on
the water's gentle corduroy.

We guess hunger pulls him
away from contemplation

as he steps forward,
scattering his wrinkled twin.

Our throats tightening
we wish him well—

long life, a full belly—
and want him to stick around,

be with us a little longer.
But our bodies signal alarm—

he's seen our kind before
and lets out four sore-

throated squawks and is gone.

White Water

Something scatters stones
    to make the water nervous
        and now all that long river
ease and calm, the soft eddy
    of daydream and memory
        scurries away. Each walrus

and whale rock, each seal's head,
    every hippo boulder juts
        to drive water to a frenzy.
Now it's all ropy foam, tresses
    combed so fast they braid
        and unbraid with fury,

then stretch down to dredge toward
    all the drowned princes coaxing
        them to shinny up to the one
great boon of air. The water
    twists to psychosis,
        blustering and pushing like

a panicked crowd driven toward
    a shrinking gate. And listen!
        That echolalia, the babble
drags us into its hysteria
    and the long message it
        delivers and then withdraws,

the one we strain for
    and almost catch, the secret
        nearly there before
a jai alai spin scoops and hurls
    it far and white and silent
        into spray, then nothing.

We walk away with emptiness
    and longing that brings us back
        again and again—watching
and feeling our beings flow downstream
    in crazy eddies with the abandon
        we've looked for all our lives.

Crows

For them their songs
are Mozart and so
they call and call

all morning for our
delight. And they
wear black as if

making fun of all
mourners. They're
smart, too, using

sticks to finagle grubs
out of stumps, even
talking if you're

fool enough to
teach them. On 101
they've got the whole

beach to scavenge
yet every time I drive
there old Heckle

and Jeckle patrol
the roadside like
they owned it, hoping I

guess for the windfall
of as Big Mac. Meanwhile
they tease drivers, flying

up just as we hit
the brakes. But what
is best about them

is their complete cocky
confidence, how on
the beach two will

horn in on a whole flock
of gulls, certain that their
fair share is more than
any lesser bird deserves.

"Finns Have Long Memories"

—L. Reino Inala

They need long memories
                    for that slow
voyage back, the Baltic rolling icy
with treachery and, worse,
the promise of the same old
starting place,
                    poverty and servitude,
that gouging harness their shoulders
remember. Not stupid
                    most pass up
the trip—they know one-way
tickets are an American's best bet.
So it starts with Ellis Island
squeezing extra
                    vowels from their names,
lightening their luggage
for the bleak journey west.
In section gangs and mines
they worked their way across
the continent,
                    finally circling like dogs
in some freezing version of home—
farms and little towns
                    in Minnesota
or Idaho where memories unclenched
relaxing like a thawing lake.
They flow toward now, riding
homesteads and land hunger,
the Depression and winter on winter
shipped over from Finland
like Care packages.
                    It's hardtack dinners
with ice and voices calling them
squarehead trash—a music they
almost like, knowing they'll

remember just who
                    said just what.
They farm the hard consonants
of their new language and never
forget how an insult
                    is spelled,
the bad grammar of each one
festering like a bad debt.

It takes some time
                    but every bastard
finally pays for a Finn's
                    long memory.
More than one smartass strawboss
found regret in a back alley
for his bad mouth.
                    But it was only
a sense of balance they were after,
liking the new phrase:
                    "You owe me one."
There were no grudges.
And it worked the other way, too:
In those Depression debts my father
paid to the penny—
                    for the little
white radio from Sears long since
spluttered into silence
and those grocery bills written off
long ago by the store owner.
Paying up,
            he bought the owner's
astonishment and his own
grim pleasure in getting things
to balance out. Sears even sent
a thank-you note.
                    Finns like this
balancing act no matter how long

it takes—those winters teach a lot
of patience.
                I remember things, too.
Some linger in the shadowy past,
others were born yesterday.
I remember both and like my father
I suggest you watch your step
and your back.
                  Remember there are
no grudges. It's more like a gene
squirreled deep inside that's in love
with balance. There's nothing I can do
about it. It forces me to set the ledger
straight. So if you owe me one
rest assured I'll make
                        it balance out
somehow, someday.

How Deadshot Reed Got His Name

We were quicksilver shadows, pocket
change dropped by the sun
dappled us like fawns.

Camouflage seemed our natural state.
We needed strangers to stay strange
and had few words

even for our few friends.
We chose our silence
and let the river do the talking,

babble enough for us
in a language we understood.
In our own way we said no

to the towns' thick grease
of worry and politics—
time clocks, mortgages, jails.

Our wilderness served up
all we wanted except the few
staples we hauled in twice a year—

salt, tobacco, a little sugar, coffee.
Otherwise potato peels made
a decent booze and we had venison

and bear, duck, pheasant, grouse
and always the fat endless salmon.
(We even tried beaver but begged

off, calling him brother.)
We grew beans and corn
and relished the winy taste

of our deep green silence
and the silence spoke through us,
saying: Leave us alone,

we get along with the animals,
killing only what we eat, wild
strawberries are sweet,

huckleberries, too.
We're sure this is a rough
version of paradise

but want no Bible thumpers here—
we had enough of their
two-faced ways in town.

We had enough of the law, too
and when those federals came
for Reed we thought they were crazy.

A war they said and Reed was drafted
to fight somewhere far off—France
someone said. He had nothing

against France and disappeared
into the dappled shadows
and it became a game.

Finally he agreed to meet
with one agent out in the open
and quickly told him he wouldn't go.

Invisible but watching
we saw the damn fool
fumble to drag out his big revolver

and Reed's 30.30 caught him
right between the eyes.
We figured that wouldn't end it—

towns are full of damn fools
and more agents came,
flashing their badges like fancy

jewelry. Reed didn't have a thing
against them, preferring elk
and deer for targets,

but what the hell,
it was him or them.
He got all three of them, too,

with no wasted bullets.
Thinking that was that he said
the others could come in and claim

the bodies but he had to drill the last one—
some cocky captain
who tried to pull a fast one

with a Derringer in his boot.
The others gave good imitations
of scalded dogs and we buried them

in unmarked graves.
But just to show that fools never learn,
they tried to draft Reed's boys

in '42 but gave up
after losing a few more
damn fools with fancy badges.

The History of Apples

It is a sad story from the start,
even here in the new world there were
once over seventy-five hundred
varieties and later about

three hundred could be found in markets.
Check your market now. How many do
you find? Their diminishment is ours—
we dwindle with them toward sameness

in all things. When did you have your last
Mammoth Black Twig? Your Spitsbergen?
There is something about lost
innocence here and a golden age—

remember Grimes Golden? The Yellow
Newton? Or the Yellow Transparent?
The Winter Banana? They speak of
the past, of open markets, daily

chopping, of neighborhoods long since gone.
Where do you buy your apples now? When
did you last taste a Gana or an
Ortley? Where have they gone? We are told

apples flourish in temperate zones—
but have they flourished?—yet they also
are very susceptible to frost.
But could frost have taken all the Wolf

Rivers, the Rhode Island Greenings? We
are told that apples are subject to
attack by many pests. Among them
are American blight and wooly

aphid and, of course, canker, silver
leaf and scab. Brown rot works them over
too, and there is also Sawfly and
Codling Moth, March Moth, Mottled Umber

Moth and, the worst, the Lacky Moth. Is
it their delicacy that has made
them disappear, unable to put
up with American blight any

longer? We can sympathize, having
weathered some of that blight ourselves yet
what about Britain? We read that it
is now impossible to obtain

pedigree stocks in England. Why? What
about Beauty of Bath, the Ribston
Pippin, the Worcester Pear, Blenheim
Orange to say nothing of the Lord

Suffield, the Stirling Castle, Cox's
Pomona, the Irish Peach and Pott's
Seedling? Given recent history
we can imagine what happened to

he Irish Peach but what of all the
others? It is a sad story, this
disappearance of apples, but no
mystery. As usual business is

at the core and saw fit to go for
Red Delicious and Winesap at the
expense of the Wagoner, Oldenburg,
Paragon, and the Fameuse. Once more

our language is thinned down by commerce
and our palates denied. We can buy
all the apples we can eat but not
the apples we want. Mainly they're ghosts

now, their mystery replaced by fakes,
exotic impostors like Balsam
Apple, Custard Apple, Rose Apple,
Star Apple, Pineapple, and of course

the Apples of Sodom. But how can
they or any of the wax numbers
at the supermarket ever in
this world be the apple of your eye?

Empty Rooms

For days after visitors leave
you hear them upstairs
moving in their rooms or find
a light on you're sure
you turned off. Other signs—
a warm cup on the sideboard,
a door closing—show
that though they're gone
they've left something more
than a toothbrush behind,
maybe small ghosts
thinner than echoes
wander the house on tiptoe
and do an amateur job
of haunting—misplacing
books, leaving a tap
running. Eventually
the little ghosts leave
and leave you with a deeper
silence than you remember.
It makes you wonder if the visitors
are lonely during the days
you keep hearing them upstairs.
Do they feel chilly, say,
as if needing a sweater?
Are their blood counts
just a shade low?
Or do they feel
they've smuggled
Something
extra home, some companion
light as a hand
towel, some contraband
atmosphere trapped in
their luggage? Maybe
this is why you feel

chilled in warm rooms
and hear doors softly closing
upstairs, forgetting it's
just the sound of your old
loneliness returning to share
these empty rooms with you.

What We Owe

Our debts whip through the night
like snakes made of
cash register tape, in and out,

hissing, then flashing
like a welder's arc,
making us forget how to sleep.

We wish they were as simple
as money even if we had some to spare.
Our owing looms with a cold inflation

as the dates of our parents' deaths
turn up again. And we face
those balloon payments

with their compound interest
of hopelessness—why didn't we
say at least once how we truly felt?

What would it have cost?
Our deathbed tries were futile,
tongues thick and it was all

too late anyway, those debts
so far past due they had long since
been written off—

but in the dark we know
they're still outstanding.
Even worse there are those near us

whose marrow we've borrowed
for sandwich spreads, whose love
we burn like kindling, whose hearts

we paved over like parking lots.
Those debts wink
their code in our blood,

our pulse something like a VCR's
12 blinking over and over—
IOU, IOU all night long.

The Traveler

After the last hero
has plucked the arrow
from his shoulder
like a toothpick

from a sandwich,
after the poisonous
drops of the late
news and the TV screen

has poured all its
light into that
tiny brilliant navel
that seals itself—

after all these things
happen and all
the houses are dark,
he goes to his cold

garage—closing
the kitchen door
carefully as the blade
of a pocketknife,

breathing the smell
of oil and metal
like the odors of sex—
and stands where

his two cars doze.
He feels his way
along the big sedan's
smooth side, hands

stroking the fender's
hip, gets in
and lets the icy
key find its cold

place. Warmed up,
the motor races,
gas pedal punched
hard to the floor,

his fingers in the steering
wheel's grooves
precise as eggs
in a carton.

He stares ahead
at the garage wall
and travels as fast
as the motor will go,

feeling the RPMs
through the thin
sole of his slipper.
Then he jumps out

and into his second
car, races its motor,
and stock-still
rides bumpy roads

into the wilderness.
Back and forth
for an hour, running
between cars,

he guns their motors
and travels—down
freeways and gravel
roads, pushing them

faster than they've
ever gone, ignoring
all limits.
Finally, he leaves

roadbeds behind
and flies from hill
to hill, over the fog
in low places,

from city to city,
sneering at all laws
and distances, free
in the dark garage.

Deadpan Elegy

He used to know so
much—had mastered
dead languages, could
sail anywhere by dead

reckoning, at billiards
he made dead shot
after dead shot, was
always dead center

at darts, could tell you
why your dead letters
went wrong, but he never
beat dead horses or wound

up in dead ends or was
kept out by dead bolts.
But for him "dead" is no
longer an adjective, of that

we are, sadly, dead certain.

At This Point

After midnight the world turns flat
and you run the risk

of falling off the edge.
So you eke your way through

the small hours
like a sleeper startled awake

in a strange motel—
lost and helpless, all sense

of direction stolen by the dark.
It's that time of life

when there is no one left
to answer your questions.

They have all gone over the edge
taking the answers

with them.
Time pulls too fast, too greedily,

weeding so many.
Now when you ask directions

you get only one—
tiptoe along that edge,

strain to keep your balance
above the night's growing hunger.

Lately

Lately, our days seem secondhand,
   even our petty legends happen
      elsewhere—to the friend of a friend.
The story, say, of the ancient woman
      begging for a ride who suddenly sprouts
   hairy legs and a machete,
or the prosthetic hook hanging from

a car door, and the wet cat dried
   in a microwave. And people swear
     such stories are true, desperate to
believe and feel some touch
      of awe in their lives, some nearness
   to the source of wonder. Never mind
that the tales are badly written—

we all want to be gullible, our
   taste arduously trained for it.
      And we're sustained it seems by
such thin rumors, such faint carbons,
     such hearsay evidence that life
   is strange and scary, adding
pepper to our bland evenings.

But nothing ever happens face-
   to-face. We live with copies
     of copies, forgeries of forgeries
surround us, our lives imitating
      bad art and then only in reproductions.
   Our clothes, our food, our music
all make our lives vicarious,

duped by special effects—slimy
   aliens spewing from the bellies
     of actors pretending to be robots
making us gag at the pretense—
     or tiny singers on distant stages

singing songs we can't hear until
we go home and listen to the tapes.

Everything grows farther and farther
    away as we use up our lives listening
        to laugh tracks and recycled
jokes of late-night hosts we're
            never even invited to meet. And we feel
        as if our own conversations were dubbed
as we exchange the newest clichés

in rooms exactly like our neighbors'.

Thieves

We stay alert for any word—
"legume" say—or an image:
Leaves scrawling the map
of Australia on the car's hood

or phrases overheard on the bus:
"Them spuds was real good."
Or, "Van Gogh only cut off
the lobe, not the whole ear."

Everything will do. We scavenge
for sounds, the heartbeat,
breathing, the seasons with their long
swirling lassos, the sea—

yes, always the sea, that vascular
rolling in, rolling out, following
the moon's instructions to the letter.
We catch birds' jumpy flight

and surefooted song. We gather it in,
the mélange of trick-or-treaters' bags,
resemblance and its fraternal twin,
the rusty hinges of Canada geese,

the umpire's hoarse definitions,
the kitchen sink. Our borders
are always open, we let it all in,
and we're always ready, light-fingered

shoplifters in the world's five and dime.

Surfaces

Think of those travelers, leftovers
from Grand Tour days, who see
only sights, guided by guidebooks

and surfaces. If some surface
is penetrated they only enter
the cool interior of a museum,

heels tapping, where more surfaces
are peered at and all history
becomes the stuff you can list

or frame—kings, battles, monuments.
Seeing Nelson's *Victory* they think
of Trafalgar Square, then maybe

of Trafalgar, saying how well
preserved the old tub is
without knowing that no surface

they touch is part of Nelson's ship.
Over the years every scrap
has been replaced, making the ship

an elaborate forgery to glorify
that other forgery—the British
Empire. Of course we all live

such deceit—the log cabin where
Lincoln wasn't born, the place in Idaho
called Indian Village built

and burned for a movie, our
own lives we keep highlighting
with lies. Such inventions give

history the props it needs, turning
fools into heroes. And it's all
intended for those travelers

of surfaces, the postcard collectors,
the sightseers who bring home
the vast currency of their

travels to spend homebound friends
provincial. But there are
ways to get behind the plaques

commemorating large-scale stupidity,
ways to peel back the surfaces
like price tags and look inside.

On the *Victory* the crew lived in
quarters cramped as a school bus,
the gun deck painted red to hide

the blood. Wandering the ship you
can feel the presence of powder
monkeys younger than your children,

and begin thinking of the victims
of kings, not kings, the victims
who died keeping decks spotless

and Nelson happy with brandy
in his room big as a tennis court.
They were the ones who lived

like cattle and whose bones
were ground to make the mortar
that holds such forgeries together.

Layers

We killed time in Southampton
watching an excavation, students
digging like dentists through
centuries into the house
of a merchant dead three hundred years,
layer by layer. All history
a series of layers, the past
going deeper and deeper, human strata
like the eons painted on desert
cliffs, each age defined as if
drawn by Mondrian. Does this
mean life is only a steady addition,
one age on top of another
as if climbing toward unreachable
stars? In Chichester Cathedral
we saw the hole poked in the floor
showing part of the Roman temple
built on the same site, dream
erected on dream. We sense
the layers of our lives, the million
anniversaries of inconsequence
going on and on like the rings
in trees circling forever, like
the skins we shed, the body ash
left in countless beds, like wallpaper
in old houses layer upon layer,
the palimpsest of the first eking
through, the pentimento of our lives
sketched there in vague outline,
like the pages of calendars—think
of them all, birthdays turning up
on one in twelve, our lives
a totting up or a subtraction?
Or just a steady layering—
another coat of paint, another
course of shingles, another roof.

Where does the past go? How many
layers of dirt cover your mother's
grave? We go back, excavators
of our lives reaching the first
lamina of hearsay just before the world
lit up and we found ourselves
alone. We go back like retracing
the rings on trees, boring inward
toward some core where it all began
in the fever of conception and then
back again like rewrapping the orange,
touring our lives from then to now,
this date, this calendar page
through the overlays of pain and bliss
in the twisting dream of our lives,
history layering over history,
all our mothers and fathers, our
unknown sisters and brothers, our shadowy
phantom lovers, king queen and serf buried
in the same grave, year eating year, our lives
built on the Roman temple before memory.

Previous titles in the Carnegie Mellon Poetry Series

Fallen from a Chariot, Kevin Prufer
Needlegrass, Dennis Sampson
Laws of My Nature, Margot Schilpp
Sleeping Woman, Herbert Scott
Renovation, Jeffrey Thomson

2006
Burn the Field, Amy Beeder
The Sadness of Others, Hayan Charara
A Grammar to Waking, Nancy Eimers
Dog Star Delicatessen: New and Selected Poems 1979–2006,
        Mekeel McBride
Shinemaster, Michael McFee
Eastern Mountain Time, Joyce Peseroff
Dragging the Lake, Robert Thomas

2007
Trick Pear, Suzanne Cleary
So I Will Till the Ground, Gregory Djanikian
Black Threads, Jeff Friedman
Drift and Pulse, Kathleen Halme
The Playhouse Near Dark, Elizabeth Holmes
On the Vanishing of Large Creatures, Susan Hutton
One Season Behind, Sarah Rosenblatt
Indeed I Was Pleased with the World, Mary Ruefle
The Situation, John Skoyles

2008
The Grace of Necessity, Samuel Green
After West, James Harms
Anticipate the Coming Reservoir, John Hoppenthaler
Convertible Night, Flurry of Stones, Dzvinia Orlowsky
Parable Hunter, Ricardo Pau-Llosa
The Book of Sleep, Eleanor Stanford

2009

Divine Margins, Peter Cooley
Cultural Studies, Kevin A. González
Dear Apocalypse, K. A. Hays
Warhol-o-rama, Peter Oresick
Cave of the Yellow Volkswagen, Maureen Seaton
Group Portrait from Hell, David Schloss
Birdwatching in Wartime, Jeffrey Thomson

2010

The Diminishing House, Nicky Beer
A World Remembered, T. Alan Broughton
Say Sand, Daniel Coudriet
Knock Knock, Heather Hartley
In the Land We Imagined Ourselves, Jonathan Johnson
Selected Early Poems: 1958-1983, Greg Kuzma
The Other Life: Selected Poems, Herbert Scott
Admission, Jerry Williams

2011

Having a Little Talk with Capital P Poetry, Jim Daniels
Oz, Nancy Eimers
Working in Flour, Jeff Friedman
Scorpio Rising: Selected Poems, Richard Katrovas
The Politics, Benjamin Paloff
Copperhead, Rachel Richardson

2012

Now Make an Altar, Amy Beeder
Still Some Cake, James Cummins
Comet Scar, James Harms
Early Creatures, Native Gods, K. A. Hays
That Was Oasis, Michael McFee
Blue Rust, Joseph Millar
Spitshine, Anne Marie Rooney
Civil Twilight, Margot Schilpp

2013

Oregon, Henry Carlile

Selvage, Donna Johnson

At the Autopsy of Vaslav Nijinksy, Bridget Lowe

Silvertone, Dzvinia Orlowsky

Fibonacci Batman: New & Selected Poems (1991-2011),
      Maureen Seaton

When We Were Cherished, Eve Shelnutt

The Fortunate Era, Arthur Smith

Birds of the Air, David Yezzi

2014

Alexandria, Jasmine Bailey

Night Bus to the Afterlife, Peter Cooley

Dear Gravity, Gregory Djanikian

Pretenders, Jeff Friedman

How I Went Red, Maggie Glover

All That Might Be Done, Samuel Green

The Wingless, Cecilia Llompart

Man, Ricardo Pau-Llosa

2015

The Octopus Game, Nicky Beer

The Voices, Michael Dennis Browne

Domestic Garden, John Hoppenthaler

We Mammals in Hospitable Times, Jynne Dilling Martin

And His Orchestra, Benjamin Paloff

Know Thyself, Joyce Peseroff

cadabra, Dan Rosenberg

The Long Haul, Vern Rutsala

Bartram's Garden, Eleanor Stanford